A Funny Thing Happened
On My Way Through Life

Fairhaven
Media

A Funny Thing Happened On My Way Through Life

Copyright© 2020 by Sheila Robertson. All rights reserved

No part of this publication may be reproduced, stored in a retrieval system or transmitted in any way by any means, electronic, mechanical, photocopy, recording or otherwise without the prior permission of the author except as provided by USA copyright law.

Published by Fairhaven Media Lynchburg TN 37352

Book design Copyright© 2020 by Fairhaven Media. All rights reserved.

Cover Illustration by Jennifer Pettyjohn
Cover and interior layout by Sheila Robertson

Published in the United States of America

ISBN-13: 978-1-947729-09-4

Humor, Storytelling

For Mama
Thanks for teaching me
to laugh at life and at myself
You're the best Mama ever
I love you

Thank you to those who helped
me edit the book:
Hubert, Mama,
Patti, Jenni and Chasity

Contents

Foot in Mouth Disease	9
Crazy Legs	13
Life with Lucy	17
Dieting by Laughter	21
Kool-aid Kid	25
A Star is Born	27
Slumber Strolling	31
Butterscotch Pudding & Hound Dogs	35
Placemats with Pokeberries	39
Snake Killer	45
Ode to a Bag of Dirt	51
Fishing Monsoon	55
Apples on the Family Tree	61
In the Pew	67
Pot of Gold	73

I once read that you need three bones to get through life, a backbone, a wishbone and a funnybone. The older I get, the more I realize this is true. You know, life is funny. No. Really. It is. I mean that literally, not in some symbolic way. As a matter of fact, if you get right down to it, life can be hilarious. All the home video clips that are caught by accident of life's funny moments prove my point.

According to Reader's Digest 'Laughter is the Best Medicine'. That's true because they got that concept from the Bible. Proverbs 17:22 says, "A merry heart doeth good like a medicine", and I'm certain the Lord knows what he's talking about. Actually, I'm convinced that I've given the Lord many a chuckle during my lifetime. There are times in the middle of laughing at life, I have to stop and shake my head at how hilarious things can be. I sometimes imagine the Lord watching me and kind of rolling His eyes with a little grin pulling at the sides of His mouth.

That's my girl. Stumbling and bumbling through life. But at least she's obedient.

Well, I'm trying to be obedient as best I know how, but, that's another subject.

Actually, its kind of funny......

Foot in Mouth Disease

    I think I first realized how funny life is when I started dating my husband. Well, that statement probably needs a little explanation. You see, it started when I was two years old and my husband was the mature age of five. That's when his family started attending our church. I say 'our' church because we were there first, and I've never let him forget that.
    We grew up in fierce competition with each other and pretty much couldn't stand one another. I always came in second during the sword drills of early church life. You know what I mean. Where all the kids stand in a line and somebody calls out a scripture. The first person that finds the scripture gets to read it out loud. Well, I LOVED to read out loud. Needless to say, I never got to because, my now husband, always beat me, and he never lets me forget that.
    So it was quite a shock to me that at the age of twenty I found myself attracted to him. We had both been away at school, but had recently returned to our home church. Low and behold, he wasn't the know-it-all jerk that he used to be. He decided that I wasn't the spoiled brat only child that he always thought that I was. (Of course his opinion of me was unfounded seeing that I could never be a spoiled brat!)
    After the attraction started, I sent a girlfriend in

the church to start hinting to him that I wanted him to ask me out. Yeah, that's probably not the brightest move, but I've never been accused of being brilliant. Not being brilliant is a big club. It took a college graduate three months to get up the nerve to ask a girl out that he had known for eighteen years! I'd still be waiting if we had been complete strangers. He later defended his delay in asking by complaining that I had picked the wrong friend to goad him into it. He didn't trust that chick because she was a busybody. Right.

He was just incredibly shy. I found this out on our first date. This was also when I realized that not only is life funny, but God has a real good sense of humor. I'm certain that on the day he decided to put us together, He elbowed a nearby angel saying, *Hey, watch this.* They're probably still laughing.

The day he asked me out started very strangely. At our church, ever so often, we would have what we called handshake or fellowship. Everybody would get up at the end of service, and while we sang a hymn we would walk around the church shaking hands with everyone. Most of the time, we all went up front and walked around the altar area singing and shaking hands. I was in front of him going up the aisle when he made a very dangerous observation out loud.

"Do you know that you've got some gray hair?"

I turned around, with what I'm sure was my best drop dead look, and said, "It's from all that wondering and worrying and waiting.....". I let that last bit kind of die off as I turned back around and continued to shake hands. Hopefully, people thought the redness of my face was due to being overcome by the Holy Spirit and not because I could bite a nail in two.

That afternoon I had to work, but I wouldn't have

gone to church anyway, because I had never gotten in the habit of attending the Sunday evening service. After all, the Wonderful World of Disney came on at 6 p.m. and there was no dragging me away from the television once that started.

    I had just gotten home from work and had dinner with my parents when the phone rang. It was him. He asked if I would like to go out to eat and maybe catch a late movie.

    "I've already eaten, but" I stared to say.

    Before I could finish my sentence, he said, "Ok. That's alright."

    Boy, he must really want to go out with me to give up that fast.

    "But, I could get a dessert," I quickly added. The thought of starting this three month process over again was more than I could take.

    "Oh, okay. That will be fine. I'll be right over."

    After dinner/dessert, we got to the theater about an hour before the next show started, so we sat in the car talking, Yeah. Right. It was more like we sat in the car and listened to me talk. His shyness had kicked in and I was drowning trying to come up with interesting things to talk about to a guy that wouldn't say anything.

    I tried sports, work, and television shows. Nothing was sparking conversation. Ah ha! I would try politics. That had to be interesting to a twenty-three year old brainiac.

    'You know, I think that new mayor that we just got is about the crooked-est man that was ever elected."

    "He's my cousin."

    "Well, that's just something I heard."

    Eye roll. Silence.

Crazy Legs

Sitting here eating my Cheetos and drinking a Sundrop, my mind wanders back to childhood. I guess that's because I've loved Cheetos and Sundrops since I was a kid. For years I thought my thumb and forefinger were going to be permanently orange.

I have two cousins that were particularly close to me during childhood, one from each side of my family. The cousin on my Mama's side grew up in Illinois. I only got to see her at Easter and Thanksgiving unless there was a special event. We had such great times together. Some of my best childhood memories involve her, and all my other cousins on Mama's side, spending time at my Granny's house in the country. For hours we would play games like: Red light Green light Dynamite Boom, Mother May I?, Hide and Seek, and Tag. Or we would walk down to the creek and throw rocks in it, or if that got too boring, we would throw somebody's shoe in the water. However, those fun times were usually limited to the two holidays.

But there was once, for some reason, she was visiting during the summer. I was around fourteen years old and she was twelve. During this trip, we were going to a water park! No. You don't understand……I said a WATER PARK! In the '70's, that was big medicine. There were very few of them in the South and it wasn't something you got to do regularly.

Oh, I forgot, some of you might be young. This was the time in history where families went on one vacation a year, if they were financially well off. Most people, like my family, went on one vacation every couple of years. So this was a big stinkin' deal. Okay, so you've got the picture now.

On top of this being a great adventure, there were sure to be cute boys there that needed to get a load of us in our brand new bathing suits.

There were many different water slides to ride and we had to try them all. Our favorite was one that actually came down a hillside weaving around rocks and through clumps of trees. We hit this one several times and decided to end the day on our favorite one. Since there were two identical slides, she suggested that we race on our last trip down. What fun!

We had to be in two different lines so we let people pass us to make sure that we arrived at the start point at the same time, side by side.

The young woman in front of me went screaming down the slide and I was next. I sat down on my mat and waited for my cousin to load the chute next to me. The chubby little boy that was in front of her took off giggling and now she was seated. We were off. We went flying down to the first turn in the slide. That's where I lost sight of her as we went in opposite directions only to join back up at the pool at the bottom.

We were both tall and thin so this should be a pretty even race. I laughed all the way to the pool anticipating us splashing into the water at the same time. I turned the last corner and was on a fast descent towards the swimming pool. I could see the other slide next to me, but I didn't see my cousin on it. I scanned the pool as I plunged in, but saw no sign of her.

Where was she?

I looked around the pool thinking she might be playing a joke on me. She was no where to be seen.

How is this possible?

We were both athletic kids, but there was no skill involved in letting gravity pull you down a hillside while you griped a rubber mat as if your life depended on it. I stood in the middle of the pool and turned back toward the slides.

Maybe she had a problem and had to get off.

And then I saw the strangest thing ever. Around the last corner came a rubber mat with a chubby little boy on it. His eyes were wide with fright and he was bent forward holding the front of his mat between his feet. Behind him, sticking up over his head, were two skinny crazy legs flailing in the wind. It was my cousin.

She had evidently been so much lighter than the chubby little boy in front of her, that she caught up with him on the slide and crashed into the back of him. Trying to avoid the crash she raised her legs up in the air. As they crashed together, this put her bottom right up against the boy's back and there was no where for her legs to go but up and over his head. I was already bent double laughing when they hit the water. The chubby little boy sank like a rock while my cousin went right over his head skipping across the pool like a small stone. So much for impressing any on-looking boys.

I've never skipped a rock since then that I didn't think about cousin crazy legs.

Life with Lucy

Lucille Ball was always my favorite actress. Every Monday night *I Love Lucy* came on at eight o'clock. Of course, they were all re-runs, but I didn't know that. Missing this program could ruin my whole week, that's how much I loved to watch her. Because I was such a picky eater, my mama would often use the threat of not getting to watch Lucy if I didn't eat a good supper. This was a nightmare for me. No Lucy?! Was she kidding?

No. She wasn't kidding. I remember one night in particular. We were having one of our regular stand-by meals which included white beans, mashed potatoes, and cornbread. I loved the beans and I loved the cornbread, but I detested the mashed potatoes. I was convinced that if the good Lord wanted us to eat mashed potatoes they would have come out of the ground that way. Potatoes were meant to be fried, period, end of sentence.

I sat crying for at least fifteen minutes at the thought of not getting to watch Lucy. In retrospect, I was probably crying because I had to eat mashed potatoes in order to watch Lucy. I know. Who doesn't like mashed potatoes, right? It was a texture thing, okay. So I heard the intro music to the show. The food had been put away, Mama had washed all the other dishes and there I sat staring down at a mound of mashed potatoes that I could hide in. I had to think fast or I might miss the entire show. Thankfully, Mama had left me an extra piece of cornbread. That's the answer! I skillfully split the cornbread in the center, hollowed it out eating the soft inside, and then I scooped as many of the mashed potatoes as I could get inside the cornbread. I placed the top back over it as if I hadn't eaten the cornbread, but had eaten a huge portion of mashed potatoes.

"Mama, have I eaten enough mashed potatoes to get to watch Lucy?" I asked as I held up my plate.

"Yes, that's enough. Just rake the rest of your plate into the garbage, put it in the sink and come in here to watch television."

Success. She would never find the potato filled cornbread and I got to start my week with Lucy.

It wasn't until I was grown that I realized that I hadn't been that clever. It was actually a 'Lucy trait' that was passed down from my Mama. She had been pulling stunts like that her whole life. It's a red letter day when you realize that you were raised by a Lucy clone.

Years later, after I was grown and gone from home, Mama got into a particularly sticky problem. She had placed several glue boards in the basement to catch German crickets. It seems they were overrun by a hoard of these nasty, cranky legged, critters. Mama liked them less than I did and that was saying something. In order to catch as many of these nightmares as possible, she didn't bend the glue boards into the small tents that they naturally make. She laid them out flat. It was just her and Daddy in the house, so she didn't have to worry about a child getting into them.

One night while Daddy was watching television, Mama decided to go to the basement to see if she had caught any crickets. She looked near the water heater, where she had left one of the boards, and sure enough there was a glue board full of crickets. What a haul!

She stood looking down at all the crickets and wondered if they were still alive or if the glue had killed them. She waved her foot gently over the top of the crickets to see if they were alive. Well, they were. They all started trying to hop and jump and she jumped with them, placing her foot straight down into the glue.

This was bad. She couldn't stand to be near them and now they were trying to hop and jump right next to her foot and she couldn't get loose. She noticed the small half inch edge around the outside of the glue board that had no adhesive on it. Perfect. If she could gently place her other foot on the edge of the board, then she would have enough leverage to pull her stuck foot loose. She eased her other foot near the bare edge of the glue board and to her horror all the crickets on the board started trying to hop again. Freaking out, she screamed and slammed her foot down. You guessed it. Lucy style. Right into the glue. Standing there about to pass out from all the hopping bugs trying to jump up and down between her feet, she started screaming.

"Bug! Bug!" (That's my Daddy's nickname.) "Come down here and help me!!"

"What's the problem?" Daddy said as he lumbered down the steps. She was interrupting *Gunsmoke* and he wasn't particularly happy about it.

"Get me loose from these things!" She pleaded in a panic as he walked through the door.

He stood there for a few seconds assessing the situation. He turned and started back up the steps as he said, "Slip your feet out of your house shoes."

Life with Lucy.

Dieting by Laughter

When I was a young (I mean younger) woman, I worked at a government facility in my hometown. There were only five women on our floor and Clara was my all time favorite co-worker. She was the secretary for one of the administrative managers in the facility, and was about the same age as my Mama. She was a warm, caring woman but an absolute hoot and we had many laughs together during the two years that I worked there. Since there were only five of us, we met each day in an empty office for lunch. It was a welcome change to get to laugh and cut up with a few girlfriends after working with men all morning.

There was one noteworthy lunchtime that I remember vividly. As we each unpacked our lunchboxes, Clara told us a story that her pastor had recently told her. It seems this happened to a friend of his and he couldn't resist passing it on to someone like Clara who would definitely appreciate the humor.

The pastor's friend and his wife had gone skiing in the nearby mountains. The husband had been skiing on several occasions, but his wife had never been skiing before and was a little nervous. He was anxious to pass on what little he knew about skiing. They donned their ski suits and carrying their skis and poles headed to the ski lift. There was a very long line that day due to new fallen snow the night before. The man and his wife took their place in the line. After a few minutes, she realized that her nervousness was playing havoc with her bladder.

"I need to go to the bathroom," she whispered to her husband.

"Don't you dare get out of line! We will have to stand here for another hour if you leave now."

She didn't want to upset her husband so she decided she could wait. Ten more minutes passed and they were nearing their time for the ski lift.

"I can't hold it any longer!" She urgently informed him.

"Look. It will only take a few minutes for us to get to the top of the ski lift and about three minutes to get back down the mountain and then you can go to the bathroom!" He wouldn't budge.

Their time came and up the mountain they went. It was a beautiful view, but it's hard to appreciate when you are so full that everything looks yellow.

When they got to the top, they immediately started down the beginners slope. She took it as long as she could. About 100 yards down the mountain, she waved her husband over to the edge of the woods.

"I can't take this any longer. I shouldn't have let you talk me out of going before we got on the lift. I'm in serious pain!! Stand here and wait for me. I'm going into the edge of the woods to pee. And don't you even try to talk me out of it," she said with determination as she awkwardly made her way into the woods on skis.

When she got what she considered to be a safe distance into the woods, she leaned her ski poles against a tree and jerked her ski suit down. She was careful to push it as far back from her as she could since her legs were still in it. She squatted down and felt the relief that can only come when a severely stretched bladder empties.

She was about halfway through this process, when she noticed her ski poles were moving. Wait a minute! They weren't moving. She was!! Her skis had broken loose possibly from the lightened load they were carrying. She grabbed for her ski poles, but missed them by inches as she continued to slide. She was starting to pick up speed and dared not stand up for fear someone would see her in this exposed state. She also didn't want to sit down in the cold snow because of her exposed state. What could she do? When she hit the edge of the woods, she was flying. Her ski suit was flapping in the wind behind her as she made her way angled across the ski slope still in a squat position.

Her husband looked up in time to see the pink flash make her way across the slope. He watched in horror as one man skiing down the slope got so excited watching the unfolding spectacle that he crashed into a tree. Another man tripped and fell, rolling head over heels down the slope.

She crashed into the snow bank on the opposite side of the slope and quickly pulled her pants and ski suit back up hoping no one had noticed.

The next morning her husband got ready to hit the slopes again.

"Aren't you coming?" he asked.

"You've got to be kidding me," she said. "No way you're getting me back up there. I'm going to sit in front of the fireplace in the lobby and read a book. Have fun."

After her husband left for the slopes, she made her way downstairs. It was a beautiful lodge with a massive stone fireplace and a roaring fire just inviting weary skiers to sit and rest. She made her way to the chair closest to the fire. Sitting on the couch near her was a man with his leg in a cast. He had it propped up on the large coffee table.

"My goodness, what happened to you?" She asked the man in the cast.

"Lady, you wouldn't believe me if I told you," he answered.

"Why wouldn't I believe you? I'd like to hear what happened to you."

"Well, yesterday I was skiing down the beginners slope trying to learn how to ski when all of a sudden, a woman came flying out of the woods on skis and she was peeing. I got so excited watching what was happening that I crashed into a tree!"

"You're right. I wouldn't believe you," she said as she got up and walked back to her room.

Pushed back from the table, bent over double laughing, five women met their diet requirements for the day. No one was able to eat lunch.

Kool-aid Kid

Did you ever realize that most of the funny things that happen to you as a teenager involve a major embarrassment? Well, they do. My life was no exception.

I've always loved Sundrop. That's a locally produced citrus soda that is heads and shoulders above all the other yellow drinks that are out there. I needed my Sundrop everyday when I got home from school. One afternoon when I got home, having looked forward all day to the traditional Sundrop, I found that we were out. Misery of miseries! What was a girl to do. Thankfully, we had grape Kool-aid so all wasn't lost. I had my Kool-aid and Cheetos as I watched a little television and then started getting my homework done.

About thirty minutes before supper was ready, my Mama asked if I wanted to drive to the small country store near our house to get a Sundrop for supper. Well, of course I did. Better than getting a Sundrop was getting to drive to the store by myself. I had just gotten my license and driving by myself was a big thrill.

I grabbed my license and keys and headed to the store like a real grown up. As I entered the store, I noticed that the sack boy was a guy that I knew. He was a year older than me and someone to impress with my newly acquired driving skills and shopping alone privileges.

I approached the check out counter in as grown-up a way as I could muster. Surely he would report to everyone at school the next day that I was out shopping and driving by myself. This would definitely win me recognition with my peers. Oh, it won me recognition all right, but not for the reasons that I wanted.

I said hello to him as I paid for my Sundrop.

"What's the matter Sheila, did you run out of Kool-aid?" He asked smiling at me.

I just smiled back perplexed. *How did he know that I had Kool-aid earlier?* I left the store and got into the car. Still wondering what he meant, I glanced in the rear view mirror as I backed out of the parking place. My question was answered.

Staring back at me in the mirror was the prettiest, most perfect purple Kool-aid moustache ever.

A Star Is Born

A have a cousin that is different from most. She and I grew up to be good friends, but we had our ups and downs through the childhood years. She was a country kid and although I was somewhat acquainted with the country life through my grandparent's farm, she was far more into it than I was. For example, as a young girl, she loved to dig up night crawlers (that's a very large, ugly worm) and chase her mama around the yard with them. Her mama was a country girl too, but there's just so much you can stand before you have to scream. She loved to feed the chickens and watch them as they scratched around in the yard. My cousin was a country kid until she moved to town when she was around nine years old. But as far as I could tell, while she was living in the country, she was about as knowledgeable a country girl as you could find. She loved the farm life and she was good at it.

Since our mamas were sisters, we spent a lot of time together. When I was almost eight years old and my cousin was close to four, my Mama was able to get us tickets to the Bozo show. What a thrill! Bozo was the pinnacle of TV watching for kids during the late '60's. It was taped and broadcast from Nashville which was just seventy miles from home. On the Bozo show, kids competed for prizes. They raced, put puzzles together, sang songs, played games and even told jokes to Bozo.

    I'm sure that I practiced running and puzzle putting together just in case I was chosen to participate. This would be the absolute best thing that happened to me that year. The day finally arrived and we drove to Nashville on a Sunday afternoon to tape the show that would air the next week. It was March 30th, but I wouldn't have been anymore excited if it had been December 25th.

    All the kids were seated in a small section of bleachers as we awaited the arrival of Bozo. Someone came out and gave us instructions and then..........there he was, in person! His white face and big red mouth mimicked the giant red wig he wore. His clothes were bright and colorful and his shoes were enormous. Did I mention Bozo was a clown?

    Soon the games began and I forgot all about the camera as I waited to be picked for anything. Then it happened. Bozo asked if anyone knew the Felix the Cat song. I shot my hand up in the air as high as I could reach and he picked me. I walked up to him as he bent over to hold the microphone and I sang the lead in song to a cartoon that would play next. I sang it perfectly. I'm sure everyone was raving about the clear perfect voice of the little seven year old girl standing there in her pretty red and white dress as she belted out the touching words to the Felix the Cat song.

    My cousin was picked for a few things for little kids and a boy cousin that had gone with us got to run a few races. And then, it happened again. I was picked for the puzzle race. The team I was on was racing against another team as we put together two giant puzzles. Mine was a Batman puzzle and I knew that we could win. When the starter buzzer sounded, I took off around to the front of the puzzle to start picking up the giant pieces and placing them in their proper place. This required bending over to get the pieces they had scattered all over the floor. Like I said, I forgot all about the camera and it was obvious when I got right in front of it and bent over. Everyone in middle Tennessee saw the pretty white panties that I was wearing under my pretty red and white dress. I didn't just bend over directly in front of the camera once, no, I had to do it several times. I'm sure the camera man still gets big laughs telling his great-grandkids that story.

But my embarrassment wasn't the highlight of the day. Not by any means. I was upstaged by my three year old cousin. Bozo asked if anyone had a joke to tell. I know that my Mama and aunt both cringed when he asked that question. You see, my young cousin was great at making up her own jokes and being the country kid that she was, you never knew what she would say. On top of that, at the ripe old age of three, she didn't have a lot of built-in filter yet.

"I've got a joke, Bozo, I've got a joke!" she waved her little hand feverishly.

Uh oh....Bozo noticed her. Run Bozo Run.

"What's your joke little girl?" He asked as he bent over in front of her with the microphone.

"What's white and has four legs?" She asked.

"I don't know little girl, what's white and has four legs?" He repeated.

"A chicken scratching in cow doodoo," she said.

Our mama's tried to hide in the bleachers, Bozo's white face turned red and my cousin made television history. She was the first three year old to ever be beeped.

Slumber Strolling

In case you missed it, this story is about sleep walking. Slumber strolling sounds so much more sophisticated and so much less boring. However, mine and Mama's sleep walking history is anything but boring.

I've always wondered what causes someone to sleep walk. Is it an over active imagination? (✓ got it) Is it exhaustion? (✓ got it) Is it too much work and not enough relaxation? (✓ got it) So far this is adding up to be a disaster.

Our family sleep walking escapades started early in life. Since they are too numerous to recount here, I will tell you a few incidents since I was grown.

I lived at home with my parents until I was married at the age of twenty-one. A few years before I left home, I was in college and evidently under a lot of stress. One night my Mama awoke with me sitting on the end of her bed looking at the window.

"Sheila, what are you doing?"

"I'm getting my picture took," I answered.

When the photographer was through, I got up and went back to my bed without waking up.

Most of the time, I start waking up near the end of the adventure, or maybe waking up ends the adventure. I'm not sure how that works. But I didn't wake up that time.

Not long after that nighttime show, the double features started. I walked into my parents bedroom in the middle of the night carrying a pair of pants and a shirt. Sound asleep of course.

"Mama, I've got my shirt and my pants here," I informed her knowing that she needed to hear this.

She sat up in the bed like a jack in the box, "What are you doing with shirt and your doll?" She asked.

At this time, I was starting to wake up, "Oh, Mama, you're asleep. Go back to bed," I said as I turned and headed back to my bed.

This waking up at the end of the adventure is something that Mama passed down to me. Evidently she was an old pro at sleep walking. It's hard to compete with the master.

She was having a nightmare one night after I had married and moved into my own house. In this nightmare, round lights were bombarding her. They were dive bombing her and she was ducking and trying to get away from them. In her dream she was down on the ground crawling trying to stay low and out of their line of sight. Her adventure came to an end when her face smacked the carpet. She woke up with her face plastered to the floor. It took a few minutes to get enough wits about her to realize what happened. She had crawled from her bedroom half way down the hallway. Her face hit the carpet because she crawled up her nightgown until it pulled her head down to the floor. We still give her a hard time about that one.

After I married and we moved to the country, I suppose all those stupid horror movies that I tried to watch as kid got the best of me. I say tried to watch because I was such a fraidy cat that I never could get all the way through a horror flick.

So, we built our house and put a beautiful balcony overlooking the living room. It ran from our bedroom on one side of the upstairs to the staircase and the other bedrooms on the other side of the upstairs. At the time we moved in, we had not yet finished the railings around the balcony. We didn't have children so it shouldn't have been a problem. Here is where the horror movies come in. My nightmare this particular night was that someone had killed my husband and slipped into bed next to me. Of course, any self-respecting woman would do exactly what I did........scream bloody murder, jump up and run!

The problem with this was that as I rounded the end of the bed and headed for the door, my husband, ripped from sleep by the screaming, came out of the bed to catch me before I hit the edge of the balcony. Guess what? In my terror induced state, it was the killer that jumped out of bed and was trying to catch me. This just added to the drama. He caught me halfway across the balcony. I collapsed in total uncontrollable fear near the stairs. Thankfully, my husband was able to convince me that it was him and not a killer and, double thankfully, I didn't fall off the balcony.

But, the highpoint of my sleep walking history was a year or two later. During the night, I started dreaming that my husband did something to irritate me. Now, I don't remember what it was, but it could've been a number of things. Lord knows, he had plenty to choose from. Because he made me mad in my dream, I decided that I would just get him back. So I got up and pulled the blanket off his side of the bed. (We learned many years ago that if we had our own blankets, we fought less. Go figure) So I pulled the blanket off of him, gathered it into my arms, and headed to the hiding place. The hiding place in my dream was a hallway that exited from our closet and led to another room. Of course there was no such place but, remember, I was dreaming. I walked with the blanket to the closet door. As I entered the closet, I stood there confused because the door that led out of the closet to the other room wasn't there. I had started waking up, a little. During this time of confusion, nature called and I went to the bathroom. I came fully awake sitting on the toilet with a blanket in my lap. I sat there for a few minutes trying to recall why I was in this position. Oh, I remember, he did something to irritate me.

Now I had a real problem. How could I get the blanket back over my husband without waking him up and having to admit my slumber strolling? As I walked back to the bed, I had an idea. I would just drop the blanket at the foot of the bed and he would think he had kicked it off. Perfect.

I gently dropped the blanket and crawled back into bed. Before I could fall asleep, I heard him mumbling. I listened intently in case he was talking in his sleep. But, he wasn't. He was fussing, and nearly cussing, because he was cold and couldn't find his blanket. Oh, did I mention it was not only the dead of night but the dead of winter? He doesn't see well without his glasses and he was feeling around at the foot of the bed for the blanket. He got up on his hands and knees and reached down into the floor at the foot of the bed.

"How did it get down here?" He fussed as he pulled it back up over him.

I smiled in the dark and made some snoring sounds. He never knew....

Butterscotch Pudding and Hound Dogs

We built our house in 1984. I mean we literally built it. At the time, my Daddy had been in construction for twenty-seven years and my Daddy-in-law had worked in construction on the side for years. So when we started to build, we had a lot of ready made help.

The only sub-contractors we hired were an electrician, a roofer, and a stone mason. Everything else was done by my Daddy, my Daddy-in-law, my Mama, my husband and myself. My Mother-in-law was more into cooking than building. As a matter of fact, both my Mama and Mother-in-law cooked lunch every Saturday for four months and brought it to the house to feed us while we worked.

It all started on July 4th. We had not yet finalized our loan at the bank so we couldn't hire anyone to dig the footer for the foundation. Having the day off, and being very anxious to get started, we decided to dig it by hand. Boy, howdy! Talk about work! By the end of the day, there were five exhausted people and one footer. But there were also half a dozen stubborn roots that wouldn't give up the fight easily. At this time, my Daddy-in-law was retired and my Mama was off on Mondays so the two of them decided they would drive out to the property and deal with those roots.

My Mama went to my in-laws house bright and early on Monday morning. She got there before my

Mother-in-law left for work to find that she had packed them a lunch for the hard work ahead. They jumped in my Daddy-in-law's old red truck and headed to the property. They started right in on the stubborn roots and were making progress when it started sprinkling. They ran for the truck.

They sat in the truck for 10-15 minutes until the rain stopped and then they went back to the task of digging roots out of the footer. It wasn't long until it started sprinkling again so they headed for the truck. Every time they went back to work, there was a little more mud to tromp through. The next time they had to run for the truck they were starting to feel the load of the extra mud on their shoes.

Sitting in the truck my Mama commented, "We look like two old hound dogs running up under the porch when it rains."

They both chuckled and waited 'til the rain stopped again. After a full seven to eight hours of this, they were exhausted and headed for home.

My Mother-in-law had just returned from work when they came dragging up to the back door. She would only let my Daddy-in-law in if he took his shoes off and she wouldn't let my Mama in at all. She said it looked like they had been fighting in the mud. They all had a good laugh over they way they looked and Mama headed home trying her best not to get mud all over her car.

The next week when my husband and I were off one day, we took my Mama and my Daddy-in-law out to lunch to thank them for 'de-rooting' our footer. We went to a local steakhouse. Now I know it's hard for you to understand this, not having known my Daddy-in-law, but the man could eat. He was 6'3" and never weighed over 165 pounds. He could eat anything he wanted, anytime he wanted, and never gain an ounce. It was no surprise to us that as soon as he was through with his steak he went looking for dessert on the salad bar. He came back to the table with a sneaky little grin on his face.

"Look what I found! My favorite, butterscotch pudding!" He smiled in anticipation.

He got a big ol' spoon of that butterscotch pudding and slowly put the whole thing in his mouth. You should have seen his face. We could tell immediately that something was wrong. He tried his best to swallow and it took at least two swallows to clear that wad he had just placed in his mouth.

"What's wrong?" I asked.

With a sickening look on his face he said, "That wasn't butterscotch pudding. It was nacho cheese sauce!"

I thought the three of us would fall out of our chairs laughing at him. It was kind of pitiful though. He was so looking forward to his dessert. After we finished giving him a hard time about it, I decided to head to the salad bar for dessert.

I started laughing again as I passed the nacho cheese sauce. Then I spied it. At the end of the bar was MY favorite, whipped lemon meringue. I got a bowl full and headed back to the table.

"What did you get?" My Daddy-in-law asked me.

"This is MY favorite, whipped lemon meringue," I said as I took my first bite. Thank the Lord my napkin was handy or I might have blown it all over the table. My lemon meringue was whipped butter.

Placemats with Pokeberries

    We live in the country. More accurately, we live in the woods in the country. When we bought our acreage, we cut a hole out of the middle for the house, cleared a winding path for a driveway and called it finished. The neighbors were excitedly waiting for us to clear trees and plant grass. Yeah right. Like I want to mow 12.5 acres for the rest of my life. And besides that, we bought the land because we loved the trees. No way were we cutting them down.
    But with the country/woodsy living came some things that I wasn't expecting. Did you know that the woods have a lot more bugs and spiders than subdivisions? Well, they do. The problem gets worse when the bugs and spiders and other sundry nightmares make their way into the house.
    Our house has a front door that opens into the great room. Directly in front of the door is the wide hallway that leads past the stairway to the kitchen. The kitchen is at the back right of the house and has a door that opens on the end of the house onto the dining porch. At one time, both doors had an old fashioned screen door that we enjoyed during the spring and fall. I'm telling you this so you can get a mental picture of one of my nightmares.
    One beautiful day in late spring we had both doors

open letting the cool breeze blow through the screen when I started hearing a strange sound. Plop, pause, plop, pause, plop pause.....

What in the world is that sound?

It stopped for a few minutes and then started again, plop, pause, plop, pause....

I began to move through the downstairs trying to locate the strange sound. It wasn't long before I came around a corner and found it. There was a huge bull frog hopping down the hall from one screen door to another. I guess he decided to take the tour and was getting his money's worth.

A couple of years later, my husband came around the same corner into the hallway to find a small snake making his way from one door to the other. Needless to say, the screen doors went bye-bye after that.

But, unfortunately, the adventures continued. Because we owned a retail business and worked until 8 p.m. each night, we had a pet door for our cats. It was an elaborate set up. The cat door was between the kitchen and the dining porch. That got the cats in and out of the house, however, the dining porch was screened. So we had to provide a way for them to get out of the screened porch to freedom. We made a little doorway about three to four feet off the ground and placed a small ledge under it. We cut the screen and inserted flaps for them to walk through to get on the other side. So they could jump up to the ledge, walk through, and jump down onto the porch. Perfect. This would keep the raccoons (or Rockys as we like to call them) out of the porch and the house. At least that was how it was supposed to work.

One night we got home a little early from work and decided to sit in the den and watch television. My chair sits where I can look down the back side of the great room directly into the kitchen. I can see the dining porch door clearly. A movement in the kitchen caught my eye. There was a very large raccoon eating from the cat's bowl. He was alternately eating and turning his head to look at me .

"Uhhh, there's a raccoon in the kitchen," I said trying not to panic.

"What!?" My husband exclaimed as he jumped to his feet.

When his recliner leg rest popped down, Rocky dived through the pet door back outside. We ran to the dining porch to discover that at some point he had ripped the screen back from one corner so that he could have a bedtime snack. Evidently, he had been coming by for a while because he knew just where to go. I wanted to get our cats in for the night and put the lock out panel in the door, but my husband assured me that since he knew we were home, Rocky wouldn't be back. Not hardly.

We sat back down to watch television again and no more than ten minutes later Rocky was sticking his head back in the pet door eyeing me and the food. We got the cats in and locked the pet door. But the adventures continued.

A week or so later we were in the kitchen getting a snack when we heard a scratching sound on the back door. The cats were inside already so we turned the lights out and eased over to the dining porch door and peered out. At the base of the door sat a Mama Rocky, a Papa Rocky and a baby Rocky. Mama and Papa were teaching Baby how to get in the house to get cat food. The little one was scratching on the pet door trying to get in. I could almost hear him saying, 'I thought you said this thing opened right up and had food in it!'

Our grand finale, show-stopping experience with Rocky happened one night after we got home from church. He must have been hard of hearing because he thought he had the house to himself until we rounded the corner into the kitchen. He was three feet from the pet door and freedom, but in his panic he forgot where he was and started running around the kitchen. My husband opened the back door, grabbed a broom and started shooing him toward the door. Rockys don't shoo very well.

He ran down the hall towards the den, made a left turn and cut across the great room. I was stationed on the staircase with a large empty box that had conveniently been sitting near the door. I was determined he wasn't getting past me up the stairs so I kept banging the box on the floor at the bottom of the stairs. He made several loops around the great room and the staircase. By this time, my husband had opened the front door and the dining room windows hoping that he would find one of these exits and hit the road.

He got a glimpse of the great outdoors and headed out the front door. Unfortunately, one of our cats was walking towards the door to see what all the commotion was about. Rocky was two feet out the door when he saw her, turned around, and ran back in! This time he turned right and started running laps around the dining room table. It took him a few minutes of hair raising frenzy to discover that the windows were open. When he realized this, he climbed up into the chair where I kept our placemats that was near the window and out he went. He was propelled off the window ledge by my husband's broom. He landed safely on the porch and made tracks for the woods.

There was just one itty bitty problem that he left behind. You see, Rockys love to munch on pokeberries. They are small purplish wild berries that grow in the South. When he crawled into the chair near the window, he evidently reached his panic/excitement maximum tolerance level. He left his partially digested pokeberry lunch all over my hand made country ruffle placemats!

Snake Killer

I have Native American ancestors on both sides of my family. My Mama's great-grandmother was half Cherokee and although I got none of her physical traits like dark hair, dark skin, and dark eyes, I'm sure that I have an Indian name. No, not Sheila. I think my Indian name would most likely be 'Snake Killer' or possibly 'Screams at Unarmed Reptiles'.

My hatred of snakes is a direct result of my fear of snakes. I came by it honest. My mama is a snake killer from way back. When I was sixteen years old, Mama came home from work one day and found my cat pawing and clawing at something up against the foundation of the house. She approached Cupcake, my cat, to see what she was playing with, expecting to see a mouse or a mole. No. Cupcake was a much better hunter than that. She had a snake pinned against the foundation blocks. Mama grabbed a hoe and helped Cupcake finish off the snake. She picked up the bloody carcass with the hoe and placed it on the wood pile for my Daddy to identify when he got home from work.

After he got home, Mama sent him outside to see what kind of snake she and Cupcake had killed. He came back a few minutes later.

"Well, what kind of snake was it?" She asked, proud of her feat.

"Hon, I couldn't swear in a court of law that it ever was a snake. I have no idea what it was," he said as he went to wash up for supper.

So with this fear and overreaction passed down from Mama, I didn't stand much of a chance.

My husband and I were working on our porch roof one hot summer day. We had been up there for a while and I was just about ready to call it a day. I glanced toward the swimming pool eagerly anticipating jumping in to cool off. I changed my mind quickly.

We have a four foot deck on the sides of the pool and a larger deck on each end. Stretched across the deck on one side of the pool with his head in the pool and his tail hanging off the other side of the deck was a big, ugly, long, gross black snake! He had to be at least five to six feet long, but to me he might as well have been a fifteen foot anaconda. I started screaming and almost fell off the porch roof. I was at least forty feet away and one story up, but I was freaking out big time.

My husband climbed down the ladder as quickly as he could, grabbed an axe propped up against the porch and took off to the pool. Of course Sammy Snake heard him coming and took off before he had a chance to whack him. The thought of jumping in to cool off was not as appealing after that. I had visions of Sammy Snake coming to get a drink while I was in the pool floating around. Or worse than that, deciding to take a dip with me. We had several more Sammy Snake sightings over the years but, we never caught him. Hopefully, he's died of old age by now.

My biggest snake problem started in a small way. The electrical meter on the outside of our house is right on the other side of the wall from our laundry room. At the time this story happened, we had a large chest type freezer that sat against the outside wall in the laundry room. Because my husband and I are both very tall, we never dry our blue jeans. We always hang them up to dry and when they get dry, we throw them on top of the freezer until we can fluff them in the dryer. I was rummaging around in the blue jean pile one day and grabbed a pair to wear. After I was dressed, I was sitting on the bottom step of the staircase tying my shoes, when my husband went into the laundry to grab a pair of jeans.

"You need to go outside," he said.

I jumped up, "What is it? Did you find a big spider?" I asked.

"No, just go outside."

"Why, what is it?" Ms. Nosey insisted on knowing.

"I found a small snake in the blue jeans!"

I started screaming before I got to the front door. I ran to the car, got inside, and locked the doors. Now, you might think that locking the doors was a strange thing to do, but you don't know my husband. He does not mind small snakes and kinda thinks they are cute. I could just see him bringing it out and opening the car door to show me how cute it was. I wasn't taking any chances, so the doors were locked. He came out with a twelve to fourteen inch chicken snake wrapped around his arm. I was lucky I didn't pass out right then and there.

That incident set the stage for the big show. I was home one day cleaning our house while Hubert was working at our store. I was in the kitchen loading the dishwasher when a shadow passed by the back door. I walked over to see what was making the shadow and I broke out in a cold sweat. Through the curtain I could see the shadow of a long snake weaving and bobbing up and down outside the door. I grabbed the .22 rifle, mustered up all the courage I could find, and headed out another door around to the back of the house. I think I started screaming when I cleared the corner of the house. The snake was draped across the electrical meter trying to look in the back door. He was four to five feet long and black as midnight. The biggest issue I had, other than being terrified, was the snake on the freezer. That previous snake had obviously gotten into the house around the electrical meter to be on the freezer inside. If little snake could get in, big snake could get in. If that happened, I would have to move.

I aimed at the snake knowing that if I hit the electrical meter I would (a) set the house on fire (which would, in fact, kill the snake) (b) ruin the meter and have to pay an enormous amount of money to have the electric company fix it or (c) all of the above and my husband would divorce me...or worse. At that moment, any of those options seemed better than having that big snake in the house.

I tried to steady myself for the shot but it was a little difficult because I was shaking with fear. I shot. Did I mention that I'm a pretty good shot? Well, evidently I am. My first shot was all snake. He fell to the ground wiggling in pain. Now I was really freaked out.

"Die! Just die! I didn't want to hurt you, I wanted to kill you!" I was screaming at the snake. I shot him three more times hitting him each time and he was still wiggling. Unfortunately, there were only four shells in the gun so I ran inside for more weapons. Now that I knew he wasn't going to get in the house, I was determined to ease his suffering. I'm not mean, just scared of snakes.

The first gun I found was my husband's Colt 38.

I ran back out determined to end this nightmare. I took aim and shot. Boy, was that thing loud. It certainly wasn't anything like shooting the .22. After three more bullets the snake was at peace.

When my husband got home, I excitedly told him the whole story.

"You shot it how many times?" He asked.

"Four shots with the .22 and four with the pistol," I was a little proud that I hadn't destroyed the electric meter, but he never even mentioned that. As a matter of fact, he wasn't near as impressed as I thought he would be.

His only reply was, "For the amount of ammunition you shot up, you could have called an exterminator!"

Men………

Ode to a Bag of Dirt

All the cousins that I've told you about so far were on my Mama's side of the family. Let me tell you about a cousin on my Daddy's side. Growing up we were inseparable. There was just 21 months difference in our age. I was the older and, of course I thought, wiser of the pair. We spent weekend nights with each other, played games, took piano lessons one after the other with the same great teacher, rode bikes, terrorized the local swimming pool and anything else we could think of. We even favored each other.

Because we looked alike, we used to let people think we were sisters. Sometimes we let them assume, sometimes we encouraged the assumption, and sometimes we just lied about it. There was one time in particular that she was very anxious for her history teacher to think that we were sisters. She had a little difficulty with 7th grade history so when the teacher innocently asked her if her daddy had been ginseng hunting lately, she told him that daddy hadn't been in a while. Of course, she wasn't really lying. Her daddy didn't hunt ginseng. My Daddy did and he and the history teacher were hunting pals. Coach Allen went through the whole year thinking she was my sister. That was hunky-dory with her because the Coach liked me and I made good grades in his class when I was in the 7th grade.

A year or so earlier, she had traveled with us to Nashville to visit my Granny on Mama's side while she was in the hospital. We had been there close to an hour, when Mama gave us permission to ride the elevator down to the lobby and get a snack. This was a real treat. Don't roll your eyes at me! I'm serious. This was a real treat. In the early 70's we didn't get to go to Nashville at the drop of a hat. There had to be a very good reason. And there were no buildings with elevators in the town we lived in. The biggest building was two stories and you were expected to hoof it up the stairs. So riding an elevator, without an adult, was an excellent adventure. We were thrilled when we got back on the elevator in the lobby and no one was on it with us.

As the doors closed, my cousin said, "I wonder what it would feel like to turn a flip on an elevator. Here, hold my coke." Famous last words.

We were going from the lobby to the 5th floor, and we had the elevator to ourselves, so there was plenty of time. We never considered that someone else could stop the elevator at the 2nd or 3rd floor and get on with us.

So I grabbed her coke, anxious to see what would happen. She squatted down on the floor and was half way through her flip, rear end stuck up in the air, when the door opened. She rolled out of the flip, stood up and stumbled against the wall.

"Wow, this elevator sure jerks me around a lot." I'll have to give her points for being quick on the explanation, but it was all I could do to keep a straight face as I handed back her coke. I could hear the thoughts of these Sunday afternoon hospital visiting people as they got on the elevator, '*Hooligans! Disgraceful!* We stared at the floor until the door opened on the 5th floor.

Years later as my 40th birthday approached, I received a lot of ribbing about being older than dirt. I figured that some of my family wouldn't be able to pass up the occasion and I was right. My 'sister' cousin came by our store on my birthday with a present and a balloon. It was just the standard Happy Birthday helium balloon but it was weighted down by an unusual object. It was a bag of dirt with a card attached explaining how old I was now. That was okay. It was all in fun, but she didn't realize how bad paybacks can be.

Twenty-one months later, I got my opportunity. I planned this one for at least a month. She worked in one of the local middle schools as a truancy officer, and both her children just happened to be attending that school that year. Her son was in 8th grade and her daughter was in 6th grade.

I took her 7th grade school annual picture and designed an entire poster around it. It was a beauty. An 11x17 poster that read, 'This is how I looked when I was your age. Today I turn 40 so stop by the office and wish me a Happy Birthday.' Down in the bottom right hand corner of the poster was some tiny, tiny print. It read, 'Yeah, give me a bag of dirt will you!' I made up about a dozen full color posters.

It just so happened that my husband and I were friends with the Principal in that school. I called him a few days before and cleared my plan with him. After school on the afternoon before her birthday, he gave me permission to slip into the school and place my posters around the office and hallways. I had the place looking good, and I must say, I was quite proud of my plan.

The morning of her birthday rolled around and she and the kids headed to the school. Being an employee, she had to get there earlier than most of the students. She parked and they started walking toward the front door.

Her daughter said, "Mama, what's that on the front door?"

She looked up. "Oh, no! It's a poster! We must have a missing child," she exclaimed in a panic as they hurried to see who was missing.

"That's ME!!" She screamed as she stood in shock looking at her 7th grade face grinning back at her. She entered the school and found them all around the glass walls of the offices. She didn't even have to read the small print at the bottom of the poster to know who had pulled this one off.

Students were popping in and out of the office all day long to wish her a happy birthday. But I didn't count on this prank being a two-fer. Right before lunch, her 8th grade son slipped into the office.

"Mama! Those things are everywhere! This is embarrassing!"

Ahhhhh........success!

Fishing Monsoon

My family loves to fish. Well, most of my family loves to fish. I like to sit and look at the water. Mama and Daddy have been fishermen for as long as I can remember. Daddy would fish anywhere there was water over ankle deep. He would fish from the shore, from a boat or from the dam. It didn't matter to him as long as he had a pole in his hand. He didn't even get upset if they weren't biting. He just loved fishing. And he was very good at it. Many times I remember him fishing all night long.

There was one time when I was just eight years old, that Daddy caught a whomper of a fish. He was fishing at the dam and had all his poles out. He decided to bait up my little 8 lb test line Zebco. He cast it over the dam wall just like his big expensive poles and settled in to wait for the big one to take a bite.

He didn't have to wait long before he saw my little pole almost go over the wall. He grabbed it and started to reel it in. He was an expert at landing big ones. He knew just how much line to give the fish as he pulled and reeled the fish into exhaustion. It took nearly an hour, but Daddy won the war and the biggest catfish anyone around our town had ever seen wound up in the back of our truck.

This fish was 33.5 lbs and over three foot long! How exciting that he caught it on my pole. I was thrilled when the local newspaper wanted a picture of Daddy holding up his fish. They even wanted me standing next to him. I thought it was so cool to get my picture in the paper until I actually saw it.

What a pair we made for the papers. Daddy had been up all night fishing and looked more like a holocaust victim than a fisherman. I just had my hair cut into a pixie and looked like little lulu standing next to him. To top it all off, the reporter captioned the picture with a phrase that still rings in my ears fifty years later. *Mr. Lawson landed a 33.5 lb catfish at Tims Ford Dam last night. Standing next to Mr. Lawson is his eight year old daughter Sheila. The fish weighs almost a third as much as Mr. Lawson's daughter.*

Now, I was no math genius in the 3rd grade, but I knew enough to know that three times 33 was awful close to 100! I was a little on the chubby side at this time during my life and I weighed 88 lbs. That's a chunky little girl for 8 years old, but I don't have to tell you how mortified I was for all my friends to think I weighed 100 lbs!! By the way, it was a man reporter. Figures. He had no sensitivity to a woman's feelings.

There was another time when I was around 10 or 11 years old that Mama decided she wanted to go fishing. It was a summer day, I was out of school and Daddy was at work so we packed up and took off to the lake. Now Mama wasn't as adventurous as Daddy so we parked near a bridge over the water and walked down to the edge of the lake. We fished for several hours and only caught one little fish. But we had fun because you can never go fishing without bringing a picnic lunch and a lot of junk food.

The whole time we were there another woman was walking up and down the shore fishing near us. She had a lot more luck than we did and had several fish by the time she was ready to go home. As she was leaving, she walked up to us.

"Would you like to have these fish I caught? It's not really enough for a meal for my family, but you could add them to what you catch and make a good supper."

"Sure!" Mama said. "But wait a minute." She grabbed a brown paper sack. "Here, put the fish in the bag."

The woman and I both looked at Mama like she had flipped her wig.

"Okay," the woman said as she dropped the fish into the bag.

Mama stepped a few feet away from the woman and said, "Now, throw them to me."

"What?" The woman asked.

"Throw them to me. I want to be able to tell my husband that I caught them without lying."

The woman threw them to Mama and was still laughing as she climbed the hill to her car.

Fast forward 45 years, Daddy is now fishing in heavenly waters but Mama and my husband still love to fish these earthly lakes and I still like looking at the water.

Recently my husband and I had been working for a couple that had a beautiful lake home. They loved to fish from their boat dock and had graciously told us to come there to fish anytime we wanted. Well, when Mama heard that, she couldn't wait to go. We picked the day, got our one day license, bait and, of course, packed a lunch with plenty of junk food.

Let me clarify something, I don't mind fishing if I

don't have to touch a worm or murder a minnow by shoving a hook through it. Niblet corn is good to use. It's not slimy and it's been dead for a while. But to most fishermen, corn is child's bait. Thankfully, my Mama and my husband love me enough not to laugh at me for using corn instead of live bait.

We arrived at the lake and made our way down the 750 steps it takes to get down to the water. Honestly, there were only about 75 steps but when you are mid 50's and your mama is late 70's, it feels like 750 steps to both of you. Of course, we had to heft it all the way down those steps with the fishing tackle, bait, snacks, drinks, sandwiches, cooler to take the enormous amount of fish we were going to catch back and a jacket, because it was mid July and might get cold before we left. Needless to say, it was several trips for me, the younger of the three fishermen.

Mama and my husband immediately started pulling perch and bream out of the lake. They had at least four or five on the stringer before I got my first piece of corn loaded up. I put my pole in and the corn would disappear. I thought it was falling off but soon I realized that a big fish about 10-11 inches long was sneaking up and grabbing it without taking the hook.

Mama and my husband continued to pull fish out right and left. They were in a heated contest while I waited for the big one. We had been there close to an hour, had eaten all our sandwiches and half the snacks when the big one bit down on the corn and hook. I jerked him out and he was at least a two pounder. Unfortunately he was a carp and ended up going right back in the lake. That was the only one I caught.....but it was the biggest.

My husband and Mama were up to 26 fish and

counting when I looked down the lake and saw what appeared to be a storm cloud.

"It's starting to cloud up, maybe we ought to pack up and head home," I said.

They weren't happy about that idea.

"Look at the cloud, it might be heading this way. Y'all have enough for a good meal, so we need to go before we get wet. I'm gonna take all this extra stuff up to the car. I think y'all need to start packing up. I'll be back in a few minutes and we will head back up to the car," I told them again.

They agreed but they still weren't happy.

I lugged as much as I could back up the mountain grumbling and complaining the whole way about old knees, aching feet and fishing.

When I got near the lake on the return trip, I noticed that cloud was a lot closer. And there sat Mama and my husband still pulling fish out of the lake.

"Why aren't y'all ready yet? Don't you see that storm?" I said as I pointed down the lake. When I looked where I was pointing, I could not believe my eyes. There was a visible wall of water moving quickly towards us. The rain was so heavy it looked like a literal wall.

"We're gonna get wet!" Mama exclaimed.

"I told y'all to get ready!" I shouted.

"We were having fun. Can we make it up to the car?" My husband said as he grabbed the cooler and his pole and vaulted up the steps two at a time.

Mama and I grabbed our poles and started after him. She was in front of me and we were climbing as fast as we could. Needless to say, we weren't breaking any stair climbing records.

My husband was out of sight by the time we got up the first 20 steps. That's when the monsoon hit. I've never been in such a rainstorm in my life. It was blowing in over my right shoulder so I tried to get up closer to Mama as we climbed hoping I was shielding her from some of the rain.

"Are you getting wet?" I asked.

"Are you kidding?!" She replied.

We both started laughing so hard that it was even more difficult to climb. By the time we reached the first level area, we were soaked to the bone and gasping for air. The basement of the house was thirty feet to our left and to the right was the next huge hill that lead to the car and the front of the house. We both took off 'running' to the left. We got up under a small portion of second story deck near a double door leading into the downstairs family room. The wind was blowing so hard that we couldn't get out of the rain even standing in the corner of the house near the door. I started banging on the door hoping they were home and could hear us.

The homeowners had been enjoying the whole show from the upstairs sunroom. They lost sight of us when we ran under the deck and couldn't figure out why we weren't at our car yet. The lady finally heard us and ran downstairs to open the door to what looked like two nearly drowned rats holding fishing poles.

I haven't been fishing since.

Apples on the Family Tree

Have you ever noticed how personality traits are passed through the family from generation to generation? Well, I didn't really appreciate this fact until I was well into mid-life. I wish I had realized this while my Granny was still living. She was a cracker jack of a Granny. I cherish the memories that I have of her, but since she's been gone, I've had the opportunity to see her through my Mama's eyes. The stories that I've heard have made it abundantly obvious that my Mama didn't fall too far from the family tree.

Raising kids during the '30's and '40's couldn't have been a picnic, but Granny made life as fun as possible. After a hard days work in the cotton fields, on top of cooking for eleven people, on top of keeping the clothes washed with a rub board, on top of keeping the house clean, picking the garden, canning vegetables, milking the cows, and at least a hundred other farm chores, Granny still had time for a good joke.

Once she managed somehow to get a face mask that looked like a skeleton. She waited til several of the girls were cleaning up the kitchen after dinner, and then she slipped outside and around to the window. She stood peeking in until she heard the screaming. My aunt was so traumatized that she still talks about that seventy years later.

Although that was a special occasion because she happened upon the mask, the other jokes to give her children a thrill were often and commonplace. One of her favorites was putting a paper sack under one of their beds with a string tied to it and run out of the room to her bed. She would wait until they were sound asleep and then she would start slowly pulling the sack. Oh, and it made a better sound if you had a few gravels in it.

There was one time when Granny had been sick for several weeks. She was tired of looking at the four walls so one cold winter afternoon, after it had snowed a little, she told a few of her girls that she wanted to get up and go rabbit hunting. The girls knew that she was telling them, in her own funny way, that she wanted to walk around outside. She didn't rabbit hunt.

They all bundled up and went out the kitchen door. Papa had been working on the foundation of the house near the back door and there was a large hole that led under the house. The girls were careful to get Granny out of the house and away from the construction area. They walked around the yard, holding on to her arms, as long as Granny could stand the cold. As they neared the back door, Granny got a little spunky.

"Just let me go and I'll slip right into the house," she said as she pulled her arms out of their grasp.

Well, she did slip, but she slipped right under the house! They pulled her back out and got her into the house. Laughing the whole way I'm sure.

When I started hearing all these Granny stories, I realized that my Mama was just like her. Mama and I have been playing jokes on each other for years.

The first running joke that I remember started when I was thirteen or fourteen years old. I used to love to get TeenBeat magazines and, being a Donny Osmond fan, I couldn't miss a single issue because they were always posting things about Donny. I'm not sure if my love for the color purple came about because of him or if I loved purple before I knew anything about Donny. Either way, I love purple and even had a purple bedroom.

But, there were others in the Teen magazines that weren't necessarily my favorites. Several of them were down right scary to me. One in particular was Alice Cooper. Now, I know that he has since become a Christian, but back in the mid '70's……..he was scary.

One of the teen magazines had a normal picture of him with the heavy strange makeup and his hair all weird. Imagine my surprise one day when I opened a book in class and found his picture staring up at me. It's a wonder I didn't scream. It didn't take long to figure out who had slipped and cut him out of the magazine. That's okay. I can take a joke.

I never said a word about Alice that day when I got home from school, but the next morning Mama got a shock when he was staring back at her as she washed the breakfast dishes. That night he was under my pillow. The next day he was in her wallet. This went on for weeks until he finally disappeared. I have no idea what happened to him. We may have worn him to a frazzle and he just ran away from home. Couldn't blame him.

The jokes and games continued throughout childhood. They seemed to slow down after I married and moved out of the house, but they never stopped. With the help of my husband, I got a real good one on Mama one day. We had a large console stereo in the '70's. You know, the big cabinet job. It was hi-fi for it's day and I nearly wore it out playing all my favorite records on it before I got my own 'hi-fi' stereo for my room. I probably ended up getting my own stereo because Mama and

Daddy were tired of listening to my pop nightmares.

One of my favorites was Bobby Sherman. He had a song on one of my albums that just absolutely drove my Mama nuts. She hated that song. I loved it. It was called *Getting Together*.

We stopped by their house one day while Mama was at work and as we were leaving we had a brainstorm. The old stereo was still operational and happened to be plugged into a plug that was operated by a switch. There was a lamp plugged into the same plug and Mama always flipped the switch when she came home from work to turn the light on. Perfect scenario for a good joke. We got old Bobby's record out and put it on the turntable with the needle at the beginning of *Getting Together* and we made sure the stereo was turned on, but the light switch was turned off.

Mama came home from work as it was getting dusk. As soon as she hit the foyer, she flipped the light switch and here goes Bobby................*Geeeeeeet-ting Together, Getting it on with a new forever.*

Mama almost got it on with a new forever because she thought she was leaving this world. She screamed thinking someone was in the house with her until she recognized Bobby's voice. Then she realized she had just been 'got' or Bobby Sherman had come over for dinner. Either way, there was a payback coming.

And then there was the day I went to get my hair cut. Strangely enough, Mama and I get our hair cut by the same guy. He and his wife own a small salon and we have become good friends over the last thirty-five years. He also likes a good joke. I was a little confused that day when he brought me a magazine and wanted me to look at some of the new hairstyles. This wasn't our usual MO. I never change my hair style and he never suggests that

I do. However, I took the magazine and started flipping through. You have got to be kidding me!! There were pictures of ME in all sorts of weird hair poses throughout the magazine. She had been very busy! There were even some pictures of her where I had 'bald-ed' her head during a college stage makeup class years earlier. Hilarious! Great joke Mama. I was laughing, the stylist and his wife were laughing. I think there were even a few other customers laughing. The payback for that one is still to come.

As you can see, my Mama is a lot like my Granny. They are both sneaky, creative, and extremely funny. The apple didn't fall too far from the tree.

But there is one Mama story that I haven't told you yet. It was a spur of the moment, it was perfectly hilarious, it was vintage Mama and it was extremely embarrassing to her fourteen year old daughter. The perfect joke.

I played city league softball. Of course, it was slow pitch. There was no such thing as fast pitch in the '70's and if there had been, I wouldn't have played. I never liked pain. I played two positions, not at the same time of course. I liked to pitch and I also loved to play first base. I was a fairly good pitcher and I was good at catching the ball, but I never was great at running, unless somebody was chasing me and then I was as fast as lightening. I never liked being chased either. This particular day was different from most. It wasn't my turn to pitch and they were short an outfielder, so they stuck me in right field. I'm sure that's because the right fielder very rarely had to run any distance to catch the ball. Most girl softball players that could get it out of the infield, hit straight away center field or pulled it to the left. Not today.

I was standing bored stiff in the right field when someone hit a bouncer right to me. Finally. I started charging the ball as it bounced my way. As I anticipated the bounce, the ball hit something in the grass and did not bounce as high as I thought it would. It scooted right under my glove. I must have tipped it because it stopped right behind me. I stepped back to grab it between my legs and lost my balance. To my mortification, I sat right down on top of that stupid ball.

And then to add insult to injury, Mama stood up in the stands and screamed, "Hatch it, Sheila!"

Where's Alice Cooper when you need him?

In the Pew

If you don't think that the Lord has a sense of humor, then you've obviously not attended church regularly in your life. Some of the funniest things can happen in church and if we let ourselves laugh at our own mistakes, then maybe more people would find church appealing. It's when we are stoic, uptight, and afraid to smile that the church gets a black eye and no one wants to listen to what we have to say. I don't mean we need to be irreverent or goofy, but we do need to acknowledge our human trait of sometimes being a little stupid, and many times being comical. So let's lighten up and look at some of the funny things I've witnessed in the house of God.

This may seem like an urban legend, but since it was my young second cousin that did it, I'm banking on the truth of it. This young second cousin of mine was a real stinker. He was very unruly and hard to handle. His mama was an extremely petite young woman, but I knew she could handle him because I witnessed her disciplining their seven year old daughter many times. She was fair but firm with the children. However, on this particular Sunday, she was at her wits end with the 2 1/2 year old boy. He was constantly trying to run to the side aisle of the church and escape. After getting his rear end swatted a few times, which never even phased him, he dropped down and started scurrying under the pews. Now all of this was being watched by his daddy who was on the stage singing in a quartet. The mama was snatching at his leg as he crawled out of reach and that's when the daddy had all he could stand. He exited the stage, went to the pew the boy was currently under, excused himself to the people being disturbed as he reached past them to snag the toddler. He put the boy under his arm like a sack of potatoes with the boys head pointing towards the back and down the aisle to the front door he went. We knew what this meant for the young scamp, and evidently he knew what it meant also. As he passed by a twelve year old girl on the back pew, the boy looked her square in the eyes and said, "Pway fo me!"

It wasn't long after this incident that I had to leave the service early one Sunday. I was a teenager and my job required that I be there by noon that day. I had to run home and change, so I left around 11:30. That was unfortunate for me, because I missed out on one of the funniest things that our church had ever seen.

Our pastor was a middle aged man and since this was an old fashioned Baptist church he, like most of our preachers, preached hard and long. He was delivering a particularly important point which had a lot of enthusiasm behind it. It also had a lot of wind behind it. The big breath of air that he expelled caught the back side of his upper plate and propelled his false teeth out of his mouth. They hit the wooden altar and bounced out onto the carpet in front of it. He jumped off the stage, over the altar, scooped them up, shoved them back in his mouth, and never missed a beat. Half the congregation busted out laughing, but the other half was looking confused. They hadn't been paying attention so they were trying to figure out what was so funny. Needless to say, the preacher had everyone's attention after that, because they were afraid that if they were un-attentive, they might miss another show.

This same pastor a few years earlier had been preaching in an outdoor camp meeting. During his sermon, he drew in a deep breath and sucked in a passing fly.

After the service, a lady came up to him and said, "Preacher, did you swallow a fly while you were preaching?"

"Yes I did Sister and I have scripture for that," he announced.

"Scripture for swallowing a fly?" She asked.

"Yes. The Word says...he was a stranger and I took him in......"

It seems that as I got older, the stories got funnier. I don't know if that's because I remember them better or if things just get funnier with age.

After I married, my husband and I were still going to church with the same group of people that we had known all our lives. Every few years our pastors changed, but we sometimes even knew them or, worse than that, we were kin to them! There was one period of a couple of years that my Daddy's brother was our pastor. At the same time, my Mama's sister was attending church with us and made a profession of faith. This made for an odd situation. My uncle on my Daddy's side was going to baptize my aunt on my Mama's side. Our baptisms were usually in a small creek that our churches had used for generations, but it was cool weather so we had to use the baptistery of another church in town.

My Aunt had been very concerned about baptism because she was slightly afraid of water. Mainly, she didn't want to get her head underwater. If you know anything about Baptists, you know that's not an option. Baptist don't sprinkle. They dunk thoroughly.

After church on the day of the baptism, she was at my parents' house. We were trying to reassure her that it would be fine. The baptism was at 2 p.m. so we took advantage of the time to try to coach her on what to do. We told her that she needed to bend at the knees when he laid her back into the water. This would keep her feet from floating out from under her as she leaned backwards. The main thing was to just relax. Have you ever noticed that when you tell someone to relax they automatically tense up?

Later that day we watched her enter the water. She was being baptized right after a ten year old boy that kicked his feet up behind him and dog paddled to the edge of the baptistery when the preacher was through with him. I guess he was in the water and, hey, why not take advantage of that and have a little fun, right?

My Uncle turned her around and gave her some quiet instructions about holding her nose before he began. He placed his right hand on her back and his left hand over her hand that was covering her nose. He gently leaned her back into the water. At this point what we didn't realize was that my Aunt didn't know to take off her pantyhose before she got in the water. That little oversight made her feet very slick on the bottom of the tub. As he leaned her backwards, she bent her knees as instructed, but it did no good. Her pantyhose feet slid out from under her. As she was going under, she grabbed my Uncle's shirt and took him with her. When she did that, it totally threw him off balance and they both went under. He was flailing around trying to get his feet under him and at the same time he was trying to get her head above water. If only we had been filming this! Everyone was laughing including my uncle. Everyone except by uncle's wife. She was mortified that we would laugh at such a serious occasion. I couldn't help it. I think the Lord Himself had to be chuckling at this one. Years have passed and it still brings a smile to my face every time I think about it.

    But the hardest time that I've ever had not laughing in church, happened just a few years ago. We are in a different church now and this new church has a full praise band. My husband and I are both on praise team and we were running a little behind one Sunday morning. For some reason, we had to drive both cars into town that morning so I hopped in the car and my husband got in the truck. As I was backing into the turn around spot in our driveway, I looked around to make sure my husband was clear before I cut the wheel into the turn around. I was looking backwards and not paying any attention to the tractor that was sitting right next to my car. I swung the wheel and WHAM! I couldn't believe I hit the tractor. What a bad start to the morning. The driver side front fender had a huge dent in it and the chains on the tractor wheel had also scratched the paint. My husband was very understanding but I was furious. I couldn't believe that I had done something so careless.

    By the time we arrived at church for praise team practice, I was in a very irritable mood. I told a few women on the team what had happened right before the Pastor called for prayer. He was on the praise team also, so we all gathered around and held hands as he asked for any prayer request. Several people spoke up before me.

"Pray for me. I'm so upset because I hit the tractor this morning on the way to church," I said.

The Pastor started praying. Imagine my surprise when he said, "Lord, please be with the man on his tractor that Sheila hit on the way to church this morning. Lord heal him," he continued.

I thought my teeth would explode trying to hold in that laugh. I was bent over double holding hands with my husband on one side and one of the women that I told what happened on the other side. I was sputtering and turning red-faced just trying to keep from ruining the rest of the prayer time. The woman next to me was also bent double trying to hold in laughter. I thought he never would finish praying so that I could roll on the floor.

As soon as he said 'Amen' five people exploded in the spirit of laughter.

Pot of Gold

I have one more story for you. It's not folksy or humorous, but it is beautiful and I hope it leaves you with a renewed since of divine love.

I love creation. I love to look at it, to walk through it, to revel in the beauty of it, and to imagine how much more beautiful it was before the fall of mankind. To me, this world is just a faint shadow of the world that awaits those who know Jesus. I think often of what awaits and it thrills me. I tell you this so you will know why this story is so special to me.

The Lord has blessed us with many unusual and moving experiences during our married life and this is probably the single most awe-inspiring one.

My husband and I are in the construction industry. For thirty-five years we have worked side by side and we wouldn't trade one minute of it for any other life that we might have had. It's been hard, but wonderful. We have a freedom that many people never know and we've also struggled in ways that many people will never know.

But, there's a bear trap in everyone's life, both self-employed and public-employed. A trap that we need to avoid at all cost. You can get so caught up in the day-to-day living that you can forget who is providing and who is ultimately in control of your life. You can get in your head what you think is the best way for your life to proceed or what is the best way for the Lord to answer your prayers. His answer doesn't always look the way you think it should and He reminded us of that in a special way one warm spring day.

We had been working all morning in a subdivision that was only a few miles from my parents house. At lunch, we decided to drive to their house to eat so that we could relax in the cool. It had rained on and off all morning with those short, furious spring showers that we get in the South, but it had stopped as we drove to lunch.

We were in our small white pickup truck driving on a country road. As we approached a large curve to the right we were ecstatic to see that the end of a beautiful rainbow was in the front yard of the house that sat in the curve. It is a rare and amazing thing to see, much less to be that close to, the end of a rainbow touching the ground.

This is where everything went into slow motion. As we started around the curve we noticed the end of the rainbow was moving towards the road. When we were at the peak of the curve, the rainbow intersected us and moved through the cab of the truck. The entire inside of the cab exploded with golden shimmering light. We were mesmerized. We looked to the left and saw it exit the road and move into the field on the other side. For once, I was truly speechless.

As I was thinking about this, I realized that the world will tell you there is a pot of gold at the end of the rainbow and our minds immediately imagine a black pot full of gold coins. And as the world usually goes, there is a smidgen of truth in that. There is a pot of gold at the end of the rainbow, but it is not earthly gold, but rather a golden light that wraps itself around you and thrills you in a way you can't imagine.

    The legend of the pot of gold is kind of like life. It doesn't always turn out the way we think or the way we dream that it will. When things don't work out, we get pouty like a three year old that didn't get their way, not understanding that His ways are high above our ways. But, for the one who follows Jesus, and truly lets Him lead, life always turns out better than we could ever dream.

Other books by Sheila Robertson

Valleys of the Shadow

Panic was rising in her throat and the smell of gunpowder was burning her nostrils. Doors opening and closing. Burst of light. Distant shouts. Blinding pain flashing through her head. The child next to her screaming. She reached to comfort the child and her arms fell limp. Waves of terror rolled over her as she realized that she couldn't move, but the fear was swimming upstream against the inner pain that threatened to drown her. *Somebody help me...*

Janice and her children broke away from suffering through years of abuse, only to find that the nightmare wasn't over, it was just beginning. Follow Janice and her family through the nightmare, the tragedy, and the years of healing, in this true account of one family's struggle against domestic abuse.

Alzheimer's....There is hope

Alzheimer's disease is among the leading causes of death in the United States. Although scientists have identified how the disease works to disable its victims, it is still a mystery why these changes occur in the brain and why the disease is increasing at such alarming rates.

Medical science doesn't yet have the answers to these questions, so author Sheila Robertson turned to the Bible for guidance. In *Alzheimer's* she uses her research to explain:

* Who is at risk for Alzheimer's disease
* The three major symptoms of the disease
* A biblical perspective on Alzheimer's symptoms
* How you can find healing and hope

Today more than ever, we need the wisdom of the mature saints of God, but Satan is robbing the church of its impact by clouding their minds with Alzheimer's. It is time to take up arms in this spiritual battle on behalf of those members of the body of Christ who need deliverance and healing.

Available ONLY through www.fairhaven.media

Fairhaven Forest Series

Fairhaven Forest The Adventure Begins

Lost in the woods after dark, kittens Fuzz and Spatz don't know which way to turn to get back to their big white house. Many of the animals that live in the woods try to give them directions, but the kittens don't listen very well.

Cold, hungry, and scared they wait out the long dark night. Soon they realize that they would already be home if they had just listened to the older and wiser animals.

Come join Fuzz and Spatz as they learn a valuable lesson about obedience and listening on their first big adventure.

Not Scary! Fairhaven Forest Monster

Fuzz and Spatz let their imaginations run away with them when they see evidence of something living under the backyard deck. Their human pets don't seem concerned that all their orange things are disappearing, but the two small kittens are very worried.

Will the orange thing eating monster find them all the way around on the front porch?

Come join Fuzz and Spatz as they learn a valuable lesson about fear and run away imaginations.

Fairhaven Forest Sugar Baby

When Fuzz and Spatz find a baby kitten in the woods, they think their dreams have come true. They always wanted a baby sister!

They soon discover that taking care of a baby is a lot more work than they expected. When the mother arrives looking for her lost baby, Fuzz and Spatz get an even bigger surprise!

Join Fuzz and Spatz on their newest adventure while they learn a valuable lesson about responsibility.

The Princesses Get a Surprise

Fuzz and Spatz are very excited when their human pets tell them they are going to get a baby brother or sister. They can hardly wait for the little black car to come back down the driveway with their new sister.

Meanwhile a long way from Fairhaven Forest, Little Bit's brothers and sisters are not very kind to him. They tell him that he's not smart enough or big enough to be 'the pick of the litter'. That's okay with Little Bit. He would rather run and play than try to impress the tall couple that came for a visit. There were six to choose from. Who would be the pick of the litter?

Fuzz and Spatz are in for a big surprise when their human pets return. What is that furry wiggling thing in the back seat of the little black car?

Join Fuzz and Spatz and learn a lesson on treating everyone the same.

Fairhaven Forest RESCUE

When Fuzz and Spatz find a baby bird in the forest, they want to help it get back to its nest, but how?

Spatz shows true courage as she volunteers to return the birdie to it's nest, but is she big enough to accomplish this by herself?

Join Fuzz and Spatz on this hair raising adventure as they learn that sometimes having courage leads us to try things that are too big for us to do alone.

Fairhaven Forest The Visitor

When Fuzz and Spatz welcome a weekend visitor, they soon discover that she has a wrong opinion about country animals.

Follow their adventure from one problem to another as the three kittens become great friends and Sissy quickly learns that it's always a good idea to spend time with someone before you decide if they are nice or not.

Sheila Robertson, author of the Fairhaven Forest series, loves to write stories based on the real life adventures of her pets and their woodland friends. She lives with her husband in Fairhaven Forest, located in southern Tennessee.

For the older child in your life an early reader chapter book series

The wood pile rolled out from under a terrified Kat as she desperately tried to maintain her balance. Bug saw what was happening and knew that she was going to get caught. He couldn't let them catch him or they were all doomed.

Best friends, June Bug and Kat, find themselves deep in a country mystery after discovering a lost shoe at the creek. Follow these young detectives as they enjoy their first adventure in *June Bug & Kat The Lost Shoe*.

June Bug held on with all his might as his hand started to slide off the slimy rope. If Kat didn't get back with help soon, he would find himself at the bottom of a very deep well.

When a ghostly figure appears across the road during the first campout of the summer, June Bug and Kat find themselves in another country mystery. Come join these best friends as they piece together clues to solve their second riddle in *Ghostly Campout*.

COMING FALL 2020
June Bug & Kat
TREASURE MAP

All these titles are available at www.fairhaven.media, amazon.com, and other fine online retailers.

The Door
Life Lessons from Valleys of the Shadow
DVD Bible Study

RELATIONSHIPS
Why are they **SO** hard?
Why do you keep making the same mistakes over and over again?

Have you ever wondered why your relationships seem to fall flat? Why do they seem to stall and never move forward?

Join Sheila Robertson in this delightful study of the four most important relationships in your life! We will be using examples from *Valleys of the Shadow,* the biography of an abused woman, and your women's ministry group will learn valuable lessons about life, love, children, and Jesus.

AVAILABLE through fairhaven.media only!

MY HOUSE

A comprehensive guide to your home's history, *My House* is a wealth of information at your fingertips. You will always have an accurate record of purchases, repairs, colors, styles and brands of the essential components of your home.

Do you wish you could remember the color you painted the Dining Room five years ago? Or maybe what the brand and color of the carpet in the Master Bedroom is? There is no more guessing with *My House.* All your pertinent information is available at anytime.

And as this book passes from homeowner to homeowner, your home's history will be preserved providing the next owner with valuable and much needed information.

So let's get started writing your home's story for people to read for years to come!

Other Fairhaven Media books
Author H.L. Robertson

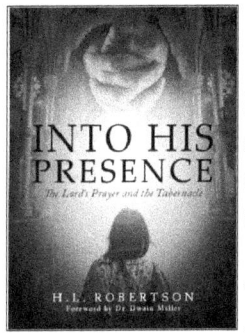

INTO HIS PRESENCE

This is a fresh and unique view of the Lord's Prayer. It is a phrase-by-phrase look at the most often repeated words ever spoken on this planet, combined with a step-by-step walk through of the Old Testament Tabernacle.

Each phrase resonates with a part of the Old Testament worship process; showing that Jesus wasn't just teaching His followers a prayer to repeat, but that He was giving them a pathway to the intimate presence of His Father. His Jewish followers would have been closely acquainted with this type of worship, and as with so many of Jesus' teachings, would have understood these words on a far deeper level than most modern Christians would recognize.

This book builds a framework of understanding for the reader, first of the Tabernacle worship system and then each phrase of the Lord's Prayer; explaining its meaning for us as believers and its significance in relation to the corresponding Tabernacle station. Also included in each chapter is a prayer of 'entering in' for that step in the journey.

Sweet Aroma

Sweet Aroma takes a unique viewpoint of the idea of our spiritual 'smell'. In this fascinating study, the author looks at the many scriptures dealing with this subject, including the aromas produced in the Tabernacle worship ceremonies, the stench of our fallen human nature in God's nostrils, and the extraordinary measures He took down through time to mask and cover our sin in order to pacify His holy anger toward us.

Next, it investigates the concept of the blessing of the firstborn as first pictured in the story of Jacob and Esau; the role of Christ as the 'firstborn son', and the implications these principles have for us today.

Finally it integrates these ideas into a framework for us to understand this revelation and to be able to proactively apply it to our everyday lives and our spiritual journey.

Bring in the Glory

Have you ever tried to enter into worship only to 'hit a wall' and find you are unable to proceed deeper into God's presence and power?

Bring in the Glory is an eye-opening look at both the worship process and the true dynamics of worship. It begins by establishing the concept of the heavenly temple and God's position in it.

This is followed by an in depth study of the character and nature of worship in heaven; including its relationship to earthly worship, the role of the angels and the future role of the believers.

It concludes with an examination of Davidic worship as a prophetic precursor to worship under the new covenant and the concept of pressing through the veil to bring the glory of God into our worship; both individually and corporately.

Sanctuary

Psalm 91 is perhaps the single most widely read, and quoted, scripture passage concerning divine protection. It is, in fact, 'stock in trade' for virtually any preacher, teacher, commentator, or writer dealing with the subject.

It is also the best writing in scripture relating to the idea of a place of intimate fellowship and communion with God. Verses one and two in particular are not only quoted with great frequency, but are inscribed on plaques, bookmarks, Christian artwork, and other paraphernalia.

This book examines this Psalm in detail along with Psalm 27, another very profound passage regarding this concept. It will also tie the 'secret place' David describes in the Psalms to other key concepts such as the tallit, the wedding canopy, Davidic worship, and Jesus' teachings on prayer.

My God is Bigger Than Nine Centimeters

Romans 12:2 states that we should prove what is the good, acceptable, and perfect will of God.

In this book I give my testimony of circumstances and situations that very much ran counter to my will and desires. However, they lead to a series of events in which nothing less than my very life was at stake.

This journey was filled with blessings and inundated with God's amazing love and care. In the end all turned out to my good despite some missteps on my part.

The DEEP WELLS Collection

The *Deep Wells Collection* is a compilation of six mini-books, previously published separately as Kindle e-books. These small, power packed books cover a wide variety of subjects ranging from the parable of the ten virgins to the symbolic meanings of wind in scripture to what Jesus wore when he was resurrected.

Each book is full of scripture references and will stimulate the reader's curiosity to draw from the 'deep wells' of God's wisdom. Blessed are those who hunger and **thirst**...

www.ingramcontent.com/pod-product-compliance
Lightning Source LLC
Chambersburg PA
CBHW052118110526
44592CB00013B/1663